The Voice of Saint Rita:
Meditations on the
Saint of Impossibilities

by

Virginia Rebata

A você a mensagem de amor da casa de
Dom Inácio desejando que os benfeitores
espirituais o ilumine e ampare.

João Teixeira de Faria
PRESIDENTE DA CASA DE DOM INÁCIO

COPYRIGHT 2015

by Virginia Rebata

Published by Bernie Bernstone

Dedicated to:

Joao Teixeira de Faria,

known as "John of God" . . .

For his tireless, life-long,
spiritual service to the
world,

which was predicted by
Saint Rita of Cascia,

when he was sixteen years
old.

Table of Contents

Acknowledgements v

Prologue ix

The Miracle of the Bees 1

Growing Up Loving the Earth 7

Embracing the Sacrament of Marriage 21

From Eager Bride to an Abused Wife 27

Forgiveness Following Tragedy 37

The Worst Pain a Mother Can Know 47

Entering the Augustinian Order in an
Impossible Way 55

Finding Peace as a Nun 75

Sharing the Passion of Christ 79

The Miracle of the Red Rose and the
Two Figs 85

Post-mortem Healing of a Carpenter 93

Post-mortem Visitation to John of God 97

Post-mortem Miracles 103

Prayers and Petitions to Saint Rita 105

Bibliography 129

Acknowledgements

My love and gratitude go first to John of God for more widely introducing Saint Rita to the world *and* to me. There are no words to adequately describe my thankfulness for his lifelong devotion to God's work and to working with the Divine Entities of Light of Abadiania. His truly benevolent mission—giving up his body as a trance medium to help heal as many people on Earth as possible—has been tireless and beyond comparison. Like Saint Rita, he has made so much healing possible, when people believed their health diagnosis to be impossible.

I thank my beloved daughter, Suzannah Jean Mullen, for always lovingly supporting me and accompanying me on my pilgrimage to Cascia and Roccaporena, Italy. She helped me realize I needed to share more about Saint Rita with the rest of the world . . . and not only as a nun, but also as a wife and mother. And, without her deeply compassionate care of me following much illness in 2013, I would have been unable to write this book.

I also thank my amazing book editor and coach, Willy Mathes, for his guidance and editing skill. Without his loving support and expertise, I would not have been able to finish this book.

I am grateful to my spiritual son and friend, Bernie Bernstone, for doing the cover and layout for this book. He is always willing to be of the kindest and utmost service in all his endeavors.

And finally, I thank my Portuguese tutor and translator, Daniel Prates, for his excellent customer service and translating expertise. I am so happy that he has helped me share the story of Saint Rita with the Portuguese-speaking people who visit John of God in Abadiania, Brazil.

Photo by Jeanne Freebody.

Prologue

I was visiting my hometown of San Francisco in 2005, walking for fun in the old Italian neighborhood below Coit Tower. I came upon a church bazaar that looked enticing—located in the basement of the Church of Saint Francis of Assisi—and I strolled in to see what spiritual treasure I might find among the religious artifacts for sale.

Among the tables full of goods, I found a small picture of a nun, praying at an altar, with a huge light beaming into her forehead, coming from a crucifix of Jesus that was hanging above the altar. There were two lovely pink roses on the floor at the nun's side, and she looked like she was in a state of bliss. I immediately knew I had to have this miniature icon of "the unknown nun," and I wondered to myself who she could be. I thought the little icon might be Italian, but I wasn't sure.

This picture would sit by my night table forever after. It would take three more years for me to meet John of God and to understand that this nun was Saint Rita of Cascia, the Saint of Impossibilities, and John of God's lifelong spiritual guide and patron. (She appeared to him when he was a teenager and told him he would lead a life of spiritual service.)

Looking back, I feel as though Saint Rita led me to John of God and the Divine Entities of Light of the Casa de Dom Inacio, where John of God does his healing in the small town of Abadiania, Brazil. She was my guiding light, steering me to my spiritual mission of sharing the divine love and healing energy of the Entities of the Casa de Dom Inacio with the rest of the world. Indeed, Saint Rita has appeared to me many times during "current," when the energy of love is clearly present during group meditation at the Casa. She has also communicated messages to me through some of my spiritual sisters at the Casa, especially Claudia Navone of Florence, Italy. On numerous occasions prior to developing this book, I was told I needed to write about who Rita of Cascia was as a saint and as a woman.

For myself, going to the Casa de Dom Inacio in 2008 in Abadiania, Brazil and meeting John of God led to much physical, emotional and spiritual healing in my life, for which I am eternally grateful. It also led me to my mission—here at the latter end of my life—of being a medium, guide and Daughter of the Casa de Dom Inacio. Since then, I feel blessed to have helped thousands of people find greater peace and powerful healing on many levels, through both John of God meditations and journeys to meet John of God at the Casa.

In 2010, I had the honor of going on a pilgrimage to Cascia, Italy, where Saint Rita lived and died as a nun, and to Roccaporena, Italy, where she was born and lived as a wife and mother. One of the miracles about Saint Rita is that, since her death in 1457, her body has not decomposed. In fact, her body lies in a glass coffin, with no sign of decay, in the Basilica of Cascia. But in spite of the legacy she leaves and her strong presence in Cascia, for some reason, I found her sweet, loving energy to be more profound in Roccaporena. My daughter, Suzannah Jean Mullen, who is a filmmaker, accompanied me on this pilgrimage and captured photos of incredible light coming from a statue of Saint Rita outside the church where she was married in Roccaporena. It is during this pilgrimage that I was inspired by Saint Rita and by my daughter to write about Saint Rita's life.

You will find here as you read about her life, Saint Rita desires to help all women who are going through strife or abuse. Her wish is to comfort people experiencing grief of any kind, particularly due to the loss of a child. She wants to uplift and inspire those who desire something more meaningful in their lives and who seek to improve their state of affairs – even when it may seem impossible. I and countless others have found all we need to do is pray to her and ask for her intercession in this or that situation. Then, God's Grace, through her, will assist us in finding our way to a more blessed life.

Saint Rita is also known as a peacemaker, so she also helps those desiring to find freedom from fear in their lives and greater peace in their families, in their communities and, most importantly, in themselves. The prayers to Saint Rita at the back of this little book can help you to pray to her. However, she also loves spontaneous prayers for her help. All we need do is ask for help from the Saint of Impossibilities!

I personally want to express my thanks to Saint Rita for all her love of those of us in the world who have suffered abuse, experienced the horrors of war, severe physical or emotional pain, or faced the loss of their children, and who have been inspired by her to seek God for solace and peace. I ask our mighty, miraculous, all merciful God and His beloved Saint Rita to bless us profoundly with greater peace within our hearts and in the world at large.

With Love and Blessings Eternally to All,

Virginia

May 22, 2015

Feast Day of Saint Rita

The Miracle of the Bees

Centuries before God made me a saint, my life began with miracles.

One of them had to do with bees. I don't remember the bees . . . I was but an infant. Yet for centuries, everyone in the village of Roccaporena, as well as literally millions living beyond its borders, have talked about an incident I once had with bees . . . to the point where it became a legend.

I was an infant lying in my basket the day the miracle of the bees occurred. My mother and father, Antonio and Amata Lotti, had gone into the rocky fields located high up above our home in the Umbrian mountains to farm. They thought they had left me secure and beyond danger, underneath a large tree, whose huge branches stretched wide and protected me from the sun. Indeed, before leaving me there, my parents gave me kisses and held my little hands before they said good-bye and went off to tend to the tomatoes, onions, eggplant and garlic. Later, as I grew, I discovered they offered constant gratitude to God for the earthly abundance they received from the land. In fact, my parents made acknowledging grace a devotional practice and passed on to me this spiritual custom of offering thanks for all things on Earth. I practiced it ever since I could remember, from about three years old on.

Soon after they left for the fields, I started to doze off and breathe deeply . . . in and out of my mouth. My breathing continued to flow slowly and heavily inward and outward. I breathed in with my mouth, and out with my mouth. In time, I started to drop into a sound sleep. Then a large group of bees arrived, flying in unison. They stayed together as a tight group, moving in and out of my mouth in unison with my breathing. They did not attack me, either individually or as a group. Instead, there was a peaceful buzzing rhythm and humming sound to their in and out movement.

Suddenly a farmer came walking swiftly by, returning from the fields back to his house, since he had cut himself deeply and he needed bandages to stop the bleeding. As he approached, he turned in my direction and saw me asleep in my basket . . . with the bees flowing in and out of my mouth! The farmer came over to rescue me, and started waving away the bees from my mouth using his injured hand. Lo and behold, the bees went away peacefully and I was left untouched. To his surprise, the farmer's injured hand was immediately healed, with not a trace left of a bloody injury.

The way I see it when I look back, so many things could have happened to cause serious harm or death to me, but they did not. The Father, who is full of grace, gave grace to me, the farmer and my parents that day.

When my parents, the Lottis, arrived on the scene shortly thereafter, they were amazed *and* mortified at what had happened. They felt terrible guilt for having left me by myself; however, they were so grateful the farmer had stopped by to save me (if I had needed it). They vowed to never put me in peril again, *and* vowed to God that they would always protect me as their precious gift from Him.

After all, they *had* wanted me for almost twelve years of attempting parenthood, but nothing they'd tried quite worked. My parents had asked and asked for me to come into the world, and had repeatedly put this prayer in God's magnanimous hands . . . until one day it was finally answered.

As you meditate, dear Ones, remember that you are always protected in God's world. Just as God protected me from the bees, He will protect you in your hour of need.

All you need do is call on His merciful, compassionate protection, and it will be so!

Growing Up Loving the Earth

I came along in 1381, exactly 100 years after Saint Francis of Assisi's birth. Actually, the town of Assisi is about 100 kilometers from Roccaporena. Because of this proximity, I have always felt a divine connection to both Saint Francis of Assisi and his soulmate in Christ, Saint Claire of Assisi.

My birthplace, Roccaporena, which has been described as a "wide expanse of rock," was perched on a large mountain about seven miles from Cascia, an ancient city in central Italy. I was born on May 22, 1381, and soon after was brought by my parents, down the winding pathway from Roccaporena to Cascia, to be baptized. Cascia was located in the province of Umbria, known as "the heart of Italy." All those present were dressed formally, as was the tradition on feast days. There in a church in Cascia, I was baptized as "Margherita," which in the language of the time signified "the pearl." My parents always told me I was their jewel, and that is why they named me "Pearl." But from the day I was born until today, I have always been known by the diminutive, "Rita."

In Roccaporena, there was a main plaza at a crossroads, where people walked and met each other for conversation, especially when the weather was warm and comfortable—which was typically in the summer and early fall. My mother would regularly take me into the square, wrapped in a blanket and tucked snuggly in my basket. Actually, she loved to take me everywhere in that basket, so I could behold the world.

As we all know, children often learn their values and behaviors from their parents. As I was growing up, my parents, Antonio and Amata Lotti (Ferri was her maiden name), were loving people, devoted to spreading peace in Roccaporena and Cascia. They were also very devout in their religious life. People came to them from throughout the region, if they had disputes about land or relationships. My parents were always able to see both sides of a situation, and their kind and thoughtful presence oftentimes enabled people to reach harmonious and peaceful resolutions. As such, they were known as the "Peacemakers."

I always felt loved by my parents, and since the time I was a baby, they perpetually told me how much they had wanted me and how I had met their every expectation. They gave me great love and affection, and there was always peace in our household—no one ever raised their voice. Physical affection, too, was part of our daily lives. This being the case, I inherited their skills and became a peacemaker in all I did.

In fact, as I was growing up, I learned to yearn for quietness and tranquility. I liked seeing people getting along with each other and cherishing harmony. I wanted to be like my parents when I grew up, and felt especially drawn to upholding the values of a peacekeeper. People told me I was patient. My parents told me I was a most obedient daughter and regularly told me how much they loved and admired me. "You are a gift from God to us," they'd often say.

I also loved to pray and was dedicated to my daily devotional prayers. I could not imagine a day without communing with God. Whenever I accompanied my mother to Cascia, I would always ask her to go to the chapel in the convent of Saint Magdalene. Many times daily, too, I prayed in my room at home, as well as at the chapel in the church of Roccaporena. We also went to Mass every week at the Church of Saint Augustine in Cascia. I prayed so

11

much because I felt and loved the company of God, who gave me inner strength. I felt like I was in the arms of a benevolent father, surrounded in a cocoon of love. For me, there was no better place to be.

The people of Roccaporena were so original, as they were perched on the mountain, as crystals emanating from the Earth. There was one main road in the town, and the church was the principal building on the main road. In spite of the large rocks, there were gardens growing outside every house, with various floral colors of white, blue, pink and red decorating the yard of each home. The red and pink roses were my favorite. I would walk around the garden of our house looking for the red and pink roses, smelling each individually, and then picking them and placing them in a vase to enjoy in my bedroom, or bring them to my mother for our kitchen. It is in these moments of walking around the garden without a care, viewing the beautiful colors and thanking Mother Earth for her harvest and beauty, that I experienced some of the most memorable and happy moments of my childhood.

My parents were both landowners and farmers. Their vocation was to tend the land and sell their crops or food products at market. As I grew older, I also learned from my parents how to tend the land. They showed me how to plant seeds, how to clean the crops, how to tend to the dirt and plants. I loved farming, as it brought me closer to the Earth, which inspired me to express even more gratitude for its many blessings and gifts. I felt so good having my hands fully in the dirt and feeling the strength from it. Even the township of Roccaporena encouraged farming—vegetables and animals were regularly given to those who wanted to engage in farming. The initial amount given to each family consisted of patches of corn, a garden of vegetables and fruits, some sheep and some goats.

As a child I would run through the neighboring fields picking up vegetables or fruits, eating them right there in the field! And then when I was in a group of people in the fields or in a garden. I would sit and sing as I ate.

The older I got, the more my parents began to bring me with

them to Cascia, a larger town about six kilometers from our village of Roccaporena. My parents would go to the main square in Cascia to sell their vegetables and fruits. I would always feel excited about going to Cascia, knowing I would experience something new each trip.

Right next to the marketplace was a convent of Augustinian nuns. I was always attracted there. The convent, too, had a garden full of vegetables and fruits, and I would often see the nuns bent on their knees tending their crops. I began to slip away whenever possible from my parents' stall to help the nuns tend their garden. Working on my hands and knees, I felt happy, knowing I was doing worthwhile work.

I began to meet and talk with these nuns who belonged to the Augustinian order—so named because they followed the spiritual practices of Saint Augustine. They were quite happy to have me help them, and seemed to enjoy my cheerful nature. I felt grateful for how loving and affectionate these women were with me and truly at home with them.

The years went by and I came to Cascia more often, spending more and more time in the company of the nuns. It was easy for me to feel drawn to the peace the nuns exhibited, particularly during their times of prayer and meditation. This sense of peacefulness, more and more, became my way of being, and reflected the upbringing I had with my parents. I liked living simply—without a lot of clothes, jewelry or material things. This made me feel free and unencumbered. And I liked living in harmony, surrounded by people speaking kindly to each other without raising their voices. I loved the affection, the kind embraces that were offered by the nuns to others and to each other. This made me feel warm and secure.

I also loved working collectively for a higher purpose, such as tending the crops to support the nuns who helped others in need in the community. You see, because of the nuns, people without food could have a healthy meal. Those who were dying would be provided with food and healthcare, as well as spiritual comfort as they died.

The more time I spent with the nuns, the more I realized, deep in my heart, that I, too, wanted to be a nun. *This will be my vocation when I grow up, I thought. I will be a servant to God, my Creator. This is what I must do.*

I had grown up loving and admiring the peaceful and loving lifestyle of the Augustinian nuns, and wanted very much to join them and to live with them as a dutiful sister and obedient daughter of the Creator. This was what my heart longed for and desired most. I loved being in the garden with them, smelling the roses and talking about Jesus and His teachings for us. I loved tending the garden and picking fresh vegetables and fruit with which to cook. And my life felt meaningful whenever I was helping the needy people of Cascia who did not have enough to eat, or who did not have clothes to protect themselves from the cold of winter. To do this work felt like an honor to me. Making vegetable soup for the hungry gave me deep satisfaction and I always asked the Father to bless the soup so that anyone who drank it would be healed and blessed.

Dear Ones, you who live on and from the Earth, do not forget to meditate with your Mother Earth. She is a giving, generous mother who provides nutrition and sustenance to her children. Do not forget to thank her and treasure her.

Embracing the Sacrament of Marriage

I was twelve years old when my parents told me they thought it was best that I not become a nun. They viewed the convent as vulnerable, and saw it was possible that warring factions of men could storm the convent at any time, demanding food and potentially hurting the nuns. My mother and father expressed their care and concerns for me, sharing their experiences as peacemakers and telling me firsthand of the terrible strife and conflicts that occurred in the countryside for the sake of power and greed.

It was a time of ongoing civil strife and continuous warfare, where young men, fueled by the desire for power and riches, relished putting on their suits of armor and heading off to do battle with nearby towns and villages, and sometimes even with their own neighbors. Cascia was no exception, as they had an ongoing feud with the larger city of Perugia—armed conflicts between the residents of both cities were constant. Many such self-made soldiers also destroyed buildings and churches. The cry of "vendetta" or "revenge" was the popular solution to many of life's challenges and conflicts. Duty to family placed heavy demands on many shoulders, drawing some to risk the punishment of exile and even death for the sake of honor.

As my parents were getting on in age, they did not want to leave this world without securing my safety.

To this end, they arranged for me to be married. Knowing they always wanted the best for me, I accepted that they had selected Paolo Mancini—a young man who came from a good Roccaporena family, headed by Ferdinand Mancini—as my husband to be. Paolo was a guard for a tower that protected Roccaporena from outside soldiers and warring men. He was physically strong and knew how to fight with both arrows and lances. He was also handsome, with bright blue eyes and dark hair. It was clear when I met him, liveliness and laughter were part of his personality. And although he was known as being "hard-headed" at times, this did not worry me, because I felt my peaceful, tranquil nature would change him in time.

Our parents both agreed we would make a good match. Paolo's parents thought my kind, mild manner would be a good balance for Paolo. My parents thought Paolo's physical strength and combat experience would protect me and keep me safe from harm.

Paolo was eighteen and I was twelve when we were betrothed to each other, but we would have to wait several more years more before we were married. Having accepted this journey in life without complaint, I began to feel more and more attached to Paolo. I even felt joyful about being his wife.

When I was fourteen years old, we married in Saint Montano's Church in Roccaporena in the year 1395. Prior to the wedding, many ceremonial traditions were practiced, as was prevalent in those times. First, Paolo sent three women with a wedding dress and a belt to my home. A few days later, he sent three men with elegant dresses and ornaments as dowry gifts. Finally, my marriage was celebrated in the custom of the times, with ten men and ten women looking on.

However, due to the prevailing religious traditions, Paolo would have to wait until I was sixteen years of age before the marriage could be consummated and I would live with him and his family. Exactly two years later, Paolo appeared at my door with numerous men behind him as his entourage. They then escorted me to my new home. I took my wardrobe, kitchen utensils and necessary belongings, and began living with Paolo and his family in Roccaporena.

Dear Ones, the union of man and woman is a beautiful and important event in life. You come together to form a family and to bear children for the world, if this is part of your calling. You come together to worship and thank God together. You come together to grow spiritually and to learn your lessons jointly. Call on me to bless your union and to help you to grow and learn through and from each other, following the will of the Father.

From Eager Bride to an Abused Wife

I looked toward my union with Paolo with great anticipation, envisioning a loving, peaceful relationship. Having had to wait four years for the bliss of living under the same roof in marriage, as the time passed slowly by, I became eager for our being together as husband and wife.

What made me feel comfortable with any physical contact with my husband was the anticipation of having not one, but a number of children. As I was resigned to marriage, having and raising children made it more bearable and acceptable in my mind. I looked forward to the day when children would arrive in my life. I pictured how they would look as a combination of the two of us. I imagined them playing on the floor, taking them for strolls in the park by the main plaza, holding and embracing them, and putting them to bed at night with prayers and songs.

Finally, two little angels, beautiful twin sons, arrived, and they gave us both great joy. We named our sons Giangiacomo and Paolo Maria. They were baptized in the Church of St. Maria della Plebe in Cascia, and each brought me all the satisfaction I had anticipated (and more). Their bubbly smiles filled my soul. Watching them crawl as they grew, listening to their laughter as they discovered the different tastes of food, silently looking on as they fell asleep in my arms—*everything* about my sons brought me joy. They fulfilled my purpose, and the purpose of my marriage.

I did not realize when I married Paolo that he did not have faith in God, and because of this I felt somewhat deceived. Prior to our marriage, during our engagement, we would go to Mass at church in both Roccaporena and Cascia. Paolo always seemed pious during these times, bowing his head, reading parts of the Bible and singing songs at Mass. Because of his enthusiasm in going to church, I felt sure he had faith in God and in the teachings of Jesus Christ. My assuredness made me happy and secure in the hands of the man my parents had chosen for me.

But my life with Paolo changed, slowly but surely, for the worst. His irascibility started to become more and more pervasive. He had always been quick-tempered, which led to outbursts of anger, but the profundity of his anger became extensive. Paolo began to come home later and later for dinner, and when he did arrive home, his breath always smelled of alcohol. Gradually his smelly skin wreaked more and more, and his anger began to get worse and worse. He would rant and rave about everything: the dinner, how I served food, how I decorated the house, how I dressed, how I wore my hair. *Nothing* satisfied him and *everything* annoyed him! Whenever he came home, he'd soon start screaming and complaining about the warring factions threatening Cascia and Roccaporena with takeover. In his mind, the men of Perugia seemed to be the worst of the common warriors. Paolo raged that these men did not know how to handle and manage weapons. He ranted about the quality of their weapons and their stupidity. He had nothing but disdain and pure hatred for the men who tried to hold Roccaporena and Cascia hostage. I felt helpless during his ranting, and could do nothing but pray quietly to myself for peace and healing of Paolo's anger and dependence on alcohol.

It was my faith that gave me strength during these times. It was God who gave me peace inside my heart and soul. I asked, too, for the strength and ability to help my husband.

Six centuries later, I see women and men are still experiencing marital abuse and violence in alarming numbers around the world. Although women tend to still be by far the greater targets of physical, sexual and emotional abuse, men, too, experience this phenomena in the modern age.

I sense that every woman or person who has found herself or himself in an abusive relationship finds it baffling and even impossible that they arrived at this place. They wonder, *How did this happen? Why am I going through this? What did I do to get here? What do I do? How do I get out of this relationship without causing harm to my children? How do I protect my children? How do I get out alive? Is this my fault? What could I have done differently? Will he or she stop? Can things get better? Should I stay or leave? If I leave, where do I go?*

We tend to have so many questions when we realize we have reached a point when we truly need help. So I call on you to ask me for help, if you find yourself in this type of troubling situation. I will intercede with God the Father and ask Him to help you. There are many, many resources available for women and children experiencing verbal abuse and/or physical violence in the home. I will help lead you to them, so you may find protection, refuge and peace, as well as a new life. Once these are in place, I will then help you to find greater peace through forgiveness. Once we can physically separate from the problem, we must work on forgiveness from a distance. This certainly does not mean we go back into abuse, but we can find lasting peace through forgiveness. While there are an increasing number of supportive resources (both public and private) for all those facing abuse, I believe there is still the same core solution I found so many centuries ago as my "out" from the pain and heartache. *My solution was to seek God.* With God, all that is impossible is possible. Having faith that all will work out in a way that is best for all: *this* is essential. When faith and prayer are infused into a difficult situation, the difficult situation turns into something we can bear. And, with continued faith, prayer, self-analysis and a willingness to follow God's guidance, we can find a way to a safe life, a peaceful life, a new life.

It is important to look back on the abusive situation and assess our part in it. What was our role? Did we give up our power? Could I have sought psychological or therapeutic assistance to address the problem? Could I have offered greater protection to my children?

Through God, we become free. We are given the path out. We are protected.

Dear Ones, call on me. Call on me, Saint Rita of Cascia. I will help you. I will be with you during your time of need. I will intercede on your behalf with God the Father, our most compassionate and magnanimous Creator, praying for your safety, protection and well-being, as well as that of your children and loved ones.

Forgiveness Following Tragedy

Throughout my growing up years, my parents had been my emotional foundation. I always felt such unconditional love from them, that I believed nothing could ever hurt me, given their ever-present protection. They had also taught me to have great faith in God, which, as I grew, became a further fortress of protection from harm. In addition, they'd given me the gift of living in and valuing peace, being a peacemaker myself, and developing a strong sense of personal stability, peace and serenity in my life.

Shortly after my marriage to Paolo, death took both my parents quickly. My mother died first, and my father followed two months later. Their passing stunned me with sadness. I was overcome with grief, unable to bear the thought of not seeing them again. As well, I was saddened they would not see my children come into the world. My heart felt broken—it actually hurt physically. And I'd cry often, sometimes weeping quietly and other times wailing with grief.

For some time, I unconsciously found myself looking for my mother in our kitchen, where she regularly would help me chop vegetables for soup. I looked for my father at our dining table, waiting for him to lead us in prayer before a meal. (He prayed so piously and gratefully to the Creator, that he filled our hearts with warmth before beginning our supper.) Put simply, life without them seemed impossible.

Gradually, though, I found the will to face the reality of their absence. I turned to God and asked that their souls would be cared for. I must say I *did* have a strong feeling they were happy, peaceful and at rest in the arms of the Creator. And on those occasions when I felt their peace, my own heart and soul gained peace. In time, I knew at the deepest level of my being that all was well with them, and they would help look after my own sons from the spirit world.

While the years went by with our sons growing up and my dedication to them and our house, I coped with all the sadness of living with a husband who raged against me, threw things at me, and said the most damaging and hurtful words to me.

During and after these rages, I turned to God, asking for peace for Paolo and peace for myself. While Paolo only seemed to rage at me and not our sons, I was thankful to God that he spared our sons. While they *did* witness their father's rages against me, at least they did not experience this themselves. For me, this was a blessing. My heart would have been much more tormented had the rages been against all three of us.

Soon, however, more tragedy struck our home.

In the year 1413, there came a day like any other. At first, I did not think it unusual for Paolo to be late again returning from work. But I became more and more preoccupied, as the hours passed late into the night and Paolo did not return. And then the men arrived at my door to give me the news of Paolo's death. My heart exploded with grief, especially when they told me he had been murdered. In spite of his difficult temper, I loved him as my husband. Once again, facing life without him seemed so impossible, that I had trouble believing what they were telling me. They said Paolo had been found below the Tower of Collegiacone, where he worked as a guard. His body had been found riddled with knife wounds. Without much more to say, the men departed and I sat down in shock at their horrific news.

Once I got over the initial shock, I collected my coat and my sons, who immediately said they *must* come with me, and we went off into the night to find Paolo. It was not a long walk to the tower, and as we neared, I caught sight of Paolo's body on the ground with blood surrounding his knife wounds. I knew immediately this murder was due to the feuding between the Mancini family and another warring family from Roccaporena, the Ciccis.

Seeing Paolo lying there, I fell to my knees and prayed for his soul, asking God to receive him into his kingdom and give him peace following such a violent and terrible end. I asked Jesus to also receive him and lead his soul as he crossed over into the world of the spirit. I knew in my heart that, in things both great and small, Jesus was the sure path to freedom of the soul and to peace.

When a few men showed up to carry Paolo's body to our house, my sons and I led them down the road, crying tears of sorrow the entire way.

I knew then I had to focus on forgiveness for Paolo's murderers. I prayed to Jesus Christ to help me forge a path to peace from this horrendous conflict. Early the next morning, I thought to myself, *What irony that my parents wanted me to marry a man for the sake of protection, who himself ended up without protection and dying a violent death.*

In the depths of my heart, I drew strength from the death of Jesus Christ. I asked for the salvation of my husband's soul by Jesus and for consolation of my grief. I also asked in prayer to be given the strength and ability to forge peace with his murderers. While I was viewed by many as "a weak female," due to my desire for peace—I felt this even from my sons—I knew that peace was the only way to practice my Christian virtue and faith. As soon as I could, I went to the family I believed was responsible for Paolo's death to speak to them of forgiveness. I knew instinctively when I arrived they were, in fact, the ones who'd killed Paolo. I felt it as they looked at me with dread. But I surprised them when I told them I had come in peace and that I asked in the name of Jesus Christ for an end to the violence and all resentments. The family thanked me for my peacefulness and I knew in my heart they had listened sincerely . . . *and* that they had been touched by the power of my forgiveness.

One of the most powerful and healing things you can do in your life, dear Ones, is to forgive. Forgiveness is the greatest gift you can give yourself, because you save yourself from resentment, worry, anger and spiritual illness. It is a most profound message taught to us by Jesus Christ. And when you practice patience, compassion and tolerance as you forgive others, you pour love into the person and into the cosmos. The result is self-healing and the healing of others.

The Worst Pain a Mother Can Know

Reasonably so, my sons were devastated by the loss of their father. While Paolo had so often ranted against me, he'd always shown remarkable restraint with our sons. He took so much pride in them, and it was returned by their honoring their strong, extroverted and masculine father. So after Paolo's murder, they immediately wanted to avenge his death, swearing in the name of their Father in heaven and in Jesus Christ they would kill their father's murderers. Being young teenagers, their reaction to their father's cruel death was not surprising, given the warring climate of the times. Both boys began to question their father's family and friends as to who the murderer or murderers might be. They focused on one family in particular, who had always had a feud against the Mancini family. My sons began to rant in the same manner as their father, yelling that the guilty party would die a torturous death and that their blood would flow in the streets of Roccaporena.

As these vindictive tirades unfolded in our household, my heart felt heavier and heavier. Murder to me was the worst type of sin possible. I believed that only our Father in heaven had the right to take a life. It was impossible to me that my sons could become murderers with blood stained, not only on their hands, but also on their souls. And, I worried they would be killed in the process of killing. As my heart deflated, I felt anxious pains in my chest. To me, taking breaths was more like taking gasps as the distress in my heart increased and my breathing became more constricted. I strived to find peace in my troubled soul. I prayed ardently to God that He take the life of my sons, rather than permit them to be murderers. I asked Him to please stop them from avenging their father's death and causing harm to those who perpetrated it. I prayed for both forgiveness and peace for all.

And then the most unexpected, horrendous tragedy occurred: both of my sons became deathly ill with a disease that was ravaging the countryside. The symptoms were very high fevers and constant nausea and dehydration. Very quickly, they were quarantined in a building at the edge of town, where other sick people with the same disease were struggling to stay alive. Each one of them had an extremely high fever and constantly vomited their interiors of phlegm, as there was nothing left inside of them.

I went to the building and sat by their side, asking God to please heal them, bless them and not take them away from me. Suddenly, my soul cried out in grief, "I can bear my own death, the death of my husband and my parents' deaths, but I cannot bear my sons' death! Please, Father, please, please heal my sons from this horrible disease!"

I prayed for my own strength, day and night, and I prayed for strength for my sons' souls. I prayed that my prior supplications to the Father, in which I asked Him to take my sons, rather than have them commit murder, not materialize. Now, I realized, *I* was the person with blood on my hands. On my knees, I humbly asked God to please forgive me. I felt lost in my own soul and my heart breaking with grief and sadness.

And then in a flash, it was all over. My sons were dead. I felt crippled by this sudden horror, as if my heart was split wide open and cast into a deep, dark hole. I cried and cried and cried without consolation. The pain and grief in my heart were greater than I could have ever imagined possible. I beseeched God in prayer to please relieve me of this dense, insufferable pain. However, I knew instinctively I had to walk down this painful road, to feel it at such a profound level, before I could slowly crawl out of it. So I sank into unspeakable grief without any close loved ones to comfort me.

Gradually, as the days went by, and then the months, and then the years, God, in His infinite mercy and His inexhaustible compassion, healed my grief. Not a day went by when I did not pray to the Holiest. Eventually, the darkness was gradually lifted and my heartache steadily lessened. And then miracle of miracles, I began to feel joy that my sons were with our Father in heaven! I felt their souls were now joyful, were now free and with the angels, Jesus Christ, our blessed Mother Mary, and under the protection and love of the eternal, magnanimous Father-Creator, God.

Dear Ones, it is through faith in our Father in Heaven and faith that the spirit world is a world of greater peace and joy, that human grief over the loss of a loved one can be overcome. Once we realize our loved ones are in a greater and higher state of being, we can let go of the loss and sadness and feel happiness for them. When we have faith that we will be reunited with loved ones once we transition, the sadness is lessened. And when we continually believe they are closer to God, then all grief can be let go and our hearts can evolve toward greater lightness and serenity.

Entering the Augustinian Order in an Impossible Way

After Paolo and my children died, I fell into a long period of grief. I gave myself over to God to do with me what He thought best. I went to Mass regularly, ardently praying for God to watch over Paolo and my sons. Truly, I missed my sons so deeply that at times I did not know what to do with myself. However, I *did* find a place of solace in the "Scoglio," one of the rugged mountain peaks of Roccaporena. This high peak, which reminded me of being in the heavens because of its height, became my refuge and place of peace. Here I prayed to my heart's content, spending many hours daily in prayer and contemplation. I asked God to remove any feelings of self-pity, deflation, deep sadness, and despair. I also asked Him to replace these sentiments with love, charity, hope, happiness and peace. I gave up my heart daily to God, that He might mend its broken pieces and convert it into a whole heart full of love for others . . . a mended heart that could be of true service to His other children.

Feeling and knowing the only way to eradicate my grief was to be of service to others, I began to work at the local hostelry, caring for strangers and travelers who had come to Roccaporena in search of shelter, food and hospitality. This work was satisfying to me, especially after losing my children. Helping young men who had lost their way or had lost money for food and shelter, was deeply rewarding.

It renewed my spirit to help them, as I envisioned I was helping my own sons. I saw the eyes of my sons in these young men's eyes. I held them and nursed them as a mother would when they were sick. And I added them to my list of prayers for others. This routine of going to the Scoglio for meditation and prayer, and then to work with those in need, slowly but surely encouraged me and gave me strength to live another day.

One day when I was deep in meditation and prayer, I felt God nudging my thoughts into the vision of being a nun. As such images began to enter my spirit and mind's eye more and more, I realized I wanted to be a nun, just as I'd desired so many years earlier when I was a girl at the tender age of twelve. As I spent more time in prayer asking God what His will was for me, I received a clear divine message that I needed to become a nun, devoted both to Him and to charity and service.

Immediately, I began to remember the times I had planted and tended the convent garden with the nuns of the Convent of Mary Magdalene at Cascia, who were of the order of Saint Augustine. While I *had* visited them often when I was young, when I married and had my sons, my visits to the convent became more infrequent. Nonetheless, the nuns were extraordinarily kind and comforting to me when my husband and sons died. Being on my own without family, I had begun to stay in greater contact with them . . . and I began to consider the nuns, with all their kindness, my new family.

I loved the thought of living a quiet life in greater seclusion from the world, a life of prayer, contemplation, meditation and service. The desire to dedicate myself totally to God arose in my heart once again and became my greatest wish. Since I had previously had such a good friendship with the nuns, I thought they would be pleased to have me as one of their own. I made my decision to meet with them and ask them for permission to join them.

When I made my way to the Convent of Mary Magdalene to speak with them, the nuns received me with love and warmth, as they always had. They asked with concern how I was doing with recovering from my grief. It pleased them to learn I was doing so much service work with needy visitors to Roccaporena and how happy I was to do this work.

I began to speak to the nuns about my real purpose in visiting them, telling them I had always wanted to be part of their religious family and was actually there to request their consideration and approval to become an Augustinian nun. Unexpectedly, the nuns were shocked and could not believe I, having been married for eighteen years, could think it would be possible for me to be a nun. Chastity was a critical part of becoming a nun, they firmly declared. I learned, however, there *were* some nuns who loved me and, because of my disposition towards spiritual obedience and service, thought I should be considered. Sentiment seemed divided between those nuns who thought I was deserving of their inclusion of me—in light of my faith, service, and advocacy for peace—and those who thought my marriage and motherhood prevented me from becoming a nun. In addition, the latter group was also concerned about the rivalries among families in Roccaporena and Cascia, and my married family's affiliation with these rivalries.

So, even though I had forgiven Paolo's murderer's and had acted as a peacemaker with his family and with many people in the community, some of the nuns still held the affiliation against me. At the conclusion of their deliberations, I was told by the Mother Superior that it was impossible for me to join their order.

Some time passed, and one evening I was kneeling by my bed, asking God to please help me to become a nun. I was meditating with Mary Magdalene, the namesake of the convent. I found myself immersed in the vision of how *she* had been a prostitute before joining the inner circle of intimate followers of Jesus Christ. She had been with *many* men as a woman "of the street." In *my* case, I had only been a faithful and devoted wife to the father of my children. I had taken the sacrament of marriage and then become a widow. I wondered, *Why should this sacrament be held against me?*

Again, I asked my Creator and His son Jesus Christ to help me in my quest to become a nun in devotion to Them. Then suddenly, I felt the most wonderful of feelings . . . as though I was being given two large, full wings, pure white in color, and about five feet in length. And then the most impossible thing happened! I was transported to the chapel of the Mary Magdalene Convent and found myself kneeling and praying at the chapel altar, instead of beside my bed!

I looked around in wonder! There were candles burning around the chapel, as though someone had been waiting for me to arrive. I looked behind me and saw three radiant men, emanating gold light and smiling at me. I had studied the lives of the saints, but was amazed to learn the names of these three Saints: Saint John the Baptist, Saint Augustine of Hippo and Saint Nicholas of Tolentino. They told me they had come to welcome me as a nun into the Augustinian Order! Given Saint Augustine of Hippo was the founder of the Augustinian order, he said he had come to lead me into a life of prayer and seclusion.

Apparently, the lit candles and hushed conversation attracted the attention of one of the nuns who had come in to see what the commotion was. She saw me standing at the altar, talking with three men surrounded in bright, golden light, as if they were part of the sun. The nun went running to wake the Mother Superior. In the process, she woke some of the other nuns, who followed the Mother Superior in a group back to the chapel. By the time they all arrived, the three saints had departed. Only I was left standing at the chapel, smiling radiantly with a gratitude so deep I felt my heart was expanding like a marvelous, illumined bubble.

The Mother Superior asked me how I had entered the convent and chapel without a key. The iron door to the convent had a huge key the size of a large fist, and the door had remained locked. This miracle, better known as an "impossible occurrence," convinced the Mother Superior and the nuns of the Mary Magdalene Convent to accept me as one of their own. Through divine intervention, God had certainly blessed me in the most extraordinary of ways!

It was no coincidence these three saints had come to answer my prayers and guide me to my new vocation as a nun, for these three were revered by the people of Cascia. John the Baptist, the cousin of Jesus Christ, continued to be honored on the hill of Cascia many decades after the small church dedicated to his memory had given way to a much larger one named in honor of Saint Augustine. It was John the Baptist who had been the great prophet who bridged the old and new testaments, announcing the eminent coming of the Messiah. He was the one who taught how to cleanse and purify one's soul through baptism with holy water. And it was Saint John the Baptist who knew himself to be but a voice calling others to prepare the way for Jesus the Messiah . . . a witness to the light. From this saint, I learned the importance of doing God's will and proclaiming the truth of the unconditional love and forgiveness taught to us by Jesus Christ. It was through him I learned to follow Christ as my savior and teacher.

My second patron, Saint Augustine of Hippo, was the spiritual father of the friars who built the church on the hill of Cascia in the 13th century. He had led a life of intense passion for the pleasures derived from wealth, fame, lustful ways and ambition, until he converted to Catholicism at the age of 32. His devout mother, who later became Saint Monica, prayed deeply for his conversion until her prayers were answered affirmatively by God. Saint Augustine was a very talented and brilliant man whose abilities as a teacher and public orator were great. He rose quickly in the Church, until he became the bishop of Hippo in Northern Africa. Augustine wrote the *"Rule"* for those who wished to follow his example as a child of God, powerfully aware of God's love and grace. He personally founded three monastic communities in North Africa, and the monks and nuns also adopted his *Rule* for communities founded throughout Africa and the Roman Empire. I would come to learn from Saint Augustine that God is at work in our lives, even in the darkest, most disappointing experiences of life. And, when we choose to do His will, regardless of "outer" circumstances, it leads us on the sure path to peace.

My third patron, Nicholas of Tolentino, was not yet a saint when I first came to know him, although he became one during my lifetime. He was canonized 141 years after his death, and became the first member of the Order of Saint Augustine to be so honored. Nicholas was born in the town of Castel Sant'Angelo, in the region known as the Marches of Italy. His birth was similar to mine, in that his parents had been barren for many years and prayed to Saint Nicholas of Bari to obtain a child. Faithful to their prayer and pilgrimage to Bari, they named their son Nicholas after him. As a young boy, he was highly influenced by a local friar preaching in the Augustinian Order, and decided to become an ordained priest of the Augustinians. Nicholas spent most of his life in Tolentino, tending the poor and sick with his warm, compassionate personality. I always loved the legend that, once in a dream, he was visited by a friar who begged for Masses to be offered for himself and his companion who were suffering in Purgatory. He then offered Mass for seven days for these souls. On the seventh Mass, he was once again visited by the friar, who thanked him for his and many others' entrance into heaven and eternal peace. I looked to him as a friend in prayer, but also as my spiritual example for helping the sick and the poor, particularly after the death of Paolo and my children.

Less than a year later, I was formally received into the community of the Augustinian nuns at the Convent of Mary Magdalene. Upon receiving the news, I gave away all my earthly possessions to the poor of Roccaporena and Cascia, and immediately felt a deep sense of freedom and peace I had heretofore never known.

At the convent, my name was entered into the roster as Margarita Mancini Fernando. On the first day there, I was clothed in a black habit, and for forty years I lived a much hidden life of prayer, obedience, penance, charity and service to the community. This life would enable me to feed the sick and poor with my sisters in the Cascia community, which gave me deep satisfaction, knowing I was following God's will and grace. My life of daily prayer and the Augustinian Order's routine filled me with quiet joy and peace. I knew then I was in the right place for my soul.

Our Father in Heaven conducts miracles on Earth every day. He answers prayers, heals the sick, and offers financial help to those in need who ask with an open, grateful heart. Dear Ones, our Father in Heaven also has his helpers in the domain of the Saints and in the angelic realms. Call on us to help you with requests that may seem impossible. You will be amazed at the miracles that can happen with faith.

Finding Peace as a Nun

I lived forty years as a nun in the Augustinian Order. My life during that period was very simple and quite ordinary, marked by a daily routine of prayer, contemplation in silence, work and charity. Inside of me, however, I was filled with faithfulness in God and a steadfast peace. As the years went by, I understood and integrated the words of Saint Paul: "the peace that surpasses all understanding."

The gentle Rule of Saint Augustine which guided our community invited us as nuns to view all life as a gift from the Father, while pursuing a deeper and more authentic intimacy with Him. I traveled this way, living a life of union with Christ through prayer and deed. Saint Augustine wrote the Rule in the fifth century, which articulated spiritual behaviors for his monks. It was later adapted for spiritual communities of women, as well. Two principles, love of God and love of neighbor, viewed as the chief commandments preached by Jesus Christ, were paramount in this monastic life I led.

Daily prayer and contemplation or meditation in silence were the rock upon which my daily routines were founded. I prayed many hours per day, in my room, in the chapel and throughout the chores of the day.

Not surprisingly, I continued to love the garden, growing vegetables and fruits, and also planting and nurturing flowers, especially the roses that always reminded me of our blessed Mother Mary. I also spent time in the kitchen preparing food for the poor and travelers who were visiting Cascia. Another chore I enjoyed was sewing and knitting clothes for the poor and needy of Cascia. We often did this as a group of sisters in unison. There was something very soothing about doing chores together for the greater good of our community. The days passed in simple, ordinary ways and in this manner, many years passed. I did my best to always practice mercy and generosity toward the poor of Cascia. And I loved my sisters so deeply and felt that we were one entity, one community... one with the Creator and one with each other.

Our faith is nourished not only when we love our Father first and foremost, but also when we love our neighbors, our brothers and sisters in our larger community. When we are helping others in need and practicing love, mercy and generosity of spirit, we are doing the will of our Father in Heaven.

Sharing the Passion of Christ

My deep love of Jesus Christ eventually guided me towards the most important thing that happened in my life. Because of my devotion to him, I dedicated much time praying to him, spending hour after hour on my knees in my room, in chapel, and in church. Every Good Friday of my life, as long as I could remember, I prayed on my knees *at least* from twelve noon to three in the afternoon—the hours Jesus was on the cross.

In the year 1442, I was already an Augustinian nun in Cascia when Good Friday arrived. I spent that sacred time on my knees in the chapel. On that day, a great orator and preacher arrived named Friar

Giacome della Marca (in English, he is known as Saint James of the Marches). He was an intimate friend and disciple of St. Bernardino of Sienna, who based his sermons on devotion to Jesus Christ. Friar Giacome was also known to combat heretics, who were prevalent at the time. That afternoon, many of our nuns from Saint Maria Magdalena's convent gathered and joined with a large crowd to listen to him in Saint Maria della Phlebe's Church. When we returned home, I went directly to the chapel to pray. I knelt before the large crucifix in the chapel and gave myself up to God and Jesus Christ.

As I prayed, I cried with gratitude for the gift that Jesus Christ had given us for relieving us and forgiving us our sins. Then I began to pray while moving into a place of great pain. I could see the crown of thorns placed over Jesus' beautiful face, and somehow felt his incomprehensible pain. This vision was so clear and brought such grief to me, as well as such a feeling of powerlessness, that I, too, felt lost with pain. I began to cry with a deep and profound sadness, and my weeping went on for hours.

I finally asked Jesus to help me to be able to share in his painful passion. I wanted to take on a portion of the tremendous burden he had been given. As I began focusing upon Jesus there on the cross, my emotional pain began to get worse and worse, becoming almost unbearable. Suddenly, I felt a shocking, physical pain piercing

81

the middle of my forehead. (This place in the forehead is known by many spiritual practitioners as the "third eye" or the opening to the soul.) I was stunned and could not move for a few seconds. Then I reached up to see what had happened to my forehead. I then realized it was a thorn stuck into my forehead that was causing my extraordinary pain. I immediately knelt down at the altar in gratitude, in pain, and in wonder.

Christ had honored me. He had answered my prayer to share in his passion and had given me part of his stigmata. I had no words to describe my gratitude and love.

This stigmata would be with me for the rest of my life, *and* it would be painful for the rest of my life. For fifteen years, this stigmata would stay on my forehead. Often it would turn into an open wound, which sometimes oozed pus. My sister nuns would often avoid me, because they said it emitted a truly unpleasant odor. However, even though this was a difficult burden at times, it was nothing compared to the total passion of my Savior, which was a spiritual gift I embraced with love and gratitude.

There is nothing comparable to the suffering of Jesus Christ on Earth. Our own trials on Earth pale in comparison to his immense Passion. When we remember this, dear Ones, we can learn to be humble, dutiful and patient as we learn our lessons during our Earthly lives.

The Miracle of the Red Rose and the Two Figs

I had been in bed for three years with an incessant hacking cough and frequent high-temperature fevers. Even more, I felt pains throughout my body, frequently in my back, though sometimes they went from my back to my hips and legs. The pain was often excruciating, and it prevented me from walking without the help of my sisters.

The day finally came when the fever took over my body and I began to feel I was slipping away to a new place. I felt the arms of God around me, holding me, caressing my hair, letting me know that the end was coming near and that I was safe. One day, my cousin, Maria Agnelli, came to visit me, as she had heard I was getting physically worse and slipping into death. She held my hand as she sat by my bedside, and asked what she could do to help me feel better. I longed to see my old garden at my parents' house in Rocaporenna. So I asked her to go to Rocaporenna and bring me a rose from my parents' garden. Maria reminded me it was January and that finding a rose in the many feet of winter snow would be impossible. But I asked her to please try and find one, returning to Roccaporena as my eyes and ears one more time.

A few days went by before Maria returned. She had gone to Roccaporena and was shocked to find one perfect red rose growing in the garden of my parents' old home.

She picked the rose and brought it back to me. My heart was lightened when I saw the magnificent ("miraculous") red rose. I breathed in its fragrant aroma and took it as a sign that the blessed Virgin Mary was with me . . . that she, too, would be receiving me soon into the kingdom of our Father. I felt surrounded in love.

A few weeks later, my cousin returned again to the convent, knowing I was preparing for my transition, I then asked her to bring me two figs from the fig tree outside my Roccaporena house, where I had lived with my sons and husband. My cousin hastened to bring me the figs, having faith they would be on the tree, having already experienced the miracle of the rose. When Maria arrived at the garden, she saw two lusciously ripe figs growing on the frozen fig tree. When she returned with them, I knew in my heart these two figs symbolized my two beloved sons and their upcoming welcome of me when I would cross the veil from this world into the next. These two symbols of the rose of love and the figs of new life, comforted my soul. I then knew deeply I was to see my beloved Christ and Father in Heaven very shortly.

Now, I felt engulfed in various shades of red, from a pink or light red to a deep, dark red. All the colors of love took my heart into an embrace, until I felt pure, divine love. The end was near and I did not fear nor fight death. I could feel all my sisters from the convent huddled around me, silently praying or quietly whispering prayers . . . which felt like a warm blanket being placed around me in a cocoon of protection. I surrendered to death and I gave myself over to the love of God the Father, of Jesus Christ, and of the blessed Mother Mary. I welcomed the love and guidance of the divine and found perfect peace, as I glided into the arms of God in 1457.

At the moment of my passing, I could feel myself being taken into pure light and warmth. And I felt then such bliss, such utter happiness and peace. Suddenly, the bells of the convent immediately began to peal, *unaided by human hands*. My soul felt so much humility, as it witnessed the people of Cascia responding to the bells by going to the convent doors to pray for my soul and celebrate my life on Earth. I knew this was all being carried out by God's infinite grace and mercy.

While I will remain silent about what I experienced after my transition, I was delighted to know that I could continue doing God's work from the spirit world, inspiring hope, love and peace on Earth. I was surprised to learn there was much conversation about me, my life, and my post-mortem appearances. These discussions occurred in the Vatican in Rome over a long period of time. In the year 1628, I was beatified by Pope Urban VII. Two-hundred and seventy-two years later, on May 22 of the Year of Jubilee, 1900, I was canonized as "Saint Rita" by Pope Leo XII. My "feast day"—or the day of celebration of my life by the Catholic Church—is now officially May 22 every year.

Dear Ones, always remember that we are spiritual beings passing through this Earth to learn from and surpass our trials and tribulations. We do our work while we are on this Earth, as well as after. If you find yourself burdened by this work, call on me to intercede with Jesus Christ and our Holiest Father. Your burdens will be lessened and even dissipated with your faith.

Post-mortem Healing of a Carpenter

After my death, my loving sisters of the convent washed me and put me in a simple wooden coffin, which was customary at the time. One of the Cascia residents who came to pay his respects was a man named Cicco Barbaro, who had been a carpenter by trade. He was no longer able to work, as a result of paralysis from a massive stroke. He sweetly prayed over my coffin and humbly said to me, "If only I were well, Sister Rita, I would have prepared a place more worthy for you to rest."

My soul immediately interceded with the Father in Heaven, and I asked that this humble man be totally healed. And indeed, very shortly, he was perfectly healed from all illness! This was my first post-mortem miracle. Cicco Barbaro was given newfound strength in his arm and hand . . . and in gratitude, he made me the most beautiful and richly decorated coffin, in which I would rest for many years.

As more and more people came to say good-bye to me and ask my intercession in their lives, my burial was perpetually postponed. So much so, that it never actually happened! Surprisingly enough, my body did not undergo the usual process of decay. It is still preserved, to this day, although I now rest in a glass coffin in the Basilica of Cascia. Many people often say my body is "perfectly uncorrupt" and that a fragrance of roses often emanates from it. However, the coffin constructed by Cicco Barbaro still resides in the Convent of Saint Mary Magdalene, situated next door to the Basilica. It should be noted the convent is now totally cloistered and unavailable to the public.

Post-mortem Visitation to John of God

At one point, I was told by God, the Highest Holiness that I must appear to a young man named Joao Teixeira de Faria, who was living humbly in Campo Grande, in the State of Mato Grosso in southern Brazil. My purpose was to encourage and uplift his spirit and to tell him he had been selected for great spiritual work and healing, work that would be felt throughout the world and encompass the great majority of his life. Many miracles would occur through his giving up of his body for higher level spirits to heal others. Young Joao was just sixteen years of age when I appeared to him in 1957. He was so dejected, hungry, lonely and saddened that he could not find manual work in spite of his best efforts to do so. His search for employment had taken him far from home. He had stopped to rest under a bridge by a river, when I joined him to tell him that God had selected him to live a life of spiritual service to the world.

My message was meant to prepare him and to assuage any fears young Joao might have had when he began to be incorporated by higher level spirits. I instructed him on many aspects of the world of the spirit during an afternoon that we spent together. And then I gave him specific instructions to go to the Spiritist center named Christ the Redeemer. When Joao dutifully arrived there, the director of the Center asked if he was Joao Teixeira de Faria, to which Joao replied that he was indeed that person. He was told that they had been waiting for him to arrive. He then fainted and was incorporated by King Solomon.

King Solomon, the ancient wise king of Israel, teacher and writer of the Bible's Proverbs, Ecclesiastics and Song of Songs, would be his first experience of this. Many other spirits, including many saints— Saint Ignatius of Loyola, Saint Francis Xavier and Saint Francis of Assisi—would follow suit. All in all, 37 higher spirits would incorporate into Joao, in order to help millions of people throughout the world. Saint Ignatius would help most in assisting Joao to begin and found the healing center located in the small town of Abadiania, Brazil, the Casa de Dom Inacio. He would guide Joao lovingly, as would I, for the rest of his life. The spirit doctors who lived hundreds of years ago in Brazil do much of the healing at the Casa, including Dr. Augusto de Almeida, Dr. Jose Valdivino, Dr. Oswaldo Cruz, Jose Pincheado and many other higher, divine spirits. What a joy it is for us to work through Medium Joao, now known as "John of God" throughout the world, to do God's healing, loving work on Earth!

When I first saw this young man, my heart radiated with love for him. His face was kind and beautiful, with his bright blue eyes and dark hair. He returned to the bridge by the river to find me the next day following his first incorporation by King Solomon. I again appeared to him, but this time in a large shaft

100

of light. He listened intently to my message, as one contemplating a serious assignment and ready to take it on. He replied by saying he accepted his mission with all of his heart and soul. In so doing, he rendered my assignment complete. And my soul has stayed with him ever since.

Now, Joao Teixeira de Faria performs his works at the Casa de Dom Inacio, the "House of Saint Ignatius of Loyola," where thousands of visitors are healed each day. The number of visitors to the Casa can vary between 2,000 and 5,000 per day, coming from all over the world and from all walks of life. I visit the Casa regularly, always blessing and empowering my protégé.

I also appear to many people who call upon me in what is known as "the current" or the loving energy found in the meditation rooms of the Casa. Oftentimes, I help bless the vegetable soup that is served daily to every last visitor in the Casa. I infuse it with love, just as I did when I walked the Earth and helped feed the poor of Cascia and Roccaporena. I help all those who call upon me with an open, loving heart and I intercede with the Creator for all those who invoke my name at the Casa and throughout the world.

Post-mortem Miracles

I have interceded thousands and thousands of times in the lives of human beings on this Earth who have petitioned me in prayer for my assistance. No one person or organization has monitored or chronicled these visitations. As part of the Catholic Church's formal process of beautifying me in 1626, a formal investigation was conducted. At that time, 51 witnesses were questioned and 76 miraculous occurrences and healings were documented. Also noted at that time was my "perfectly uncorrupt" body and the scent of roses that emanated from it, which still remains the same to this day.

My Father in Heaven continues to permit me to work on the Earth, interceding with prayers of love, consolation and healing, especially when situations seem impossible to the human heart. What a pure blessing it is to make life possible when it seems impossible on Earth! Thank you, my beloved Jesus Christ! Thank you almighty, holy and miraculous Father for conducting miracles when my soul asks for them!

Prayers and Petitions to Saint Rita

Prayer for Cessation of Spousal Abuse

Heavenly Saint Rita,

I call upon you, Mother Rita, to help me in this difficult domestic situation I am in. I ask you to do the impossible and bless each and every one of us involved, with peace, harmony and safety. I ask that all abuse be dissipated. I ask that all anger, addiction and negative energy be removed from the situation. Finally, I pray to you for full protection and safety for me and all my loved ones involved.

In the name of Jesus Christ and Mother Mary.

Prayer for Loss of Children

Heavenly Saint Rita,

I call upon you, Mother Rita, to help me in the heart-breaking loss or separation from my children. I ask you to do the impossible and give me consolation and peace. I ask you to bless my child/children and place him/her firmly in the loving arms of God the Father. I ask that I be relieved of all grief, sadness and pain. I ask that my child/children's heart/s and soul/s be eternally protected and blessed by the Father.

In the name of Jesus Christ and Mother Mary.

Novena of the Catholic Church

A Novena is an Italian term that refers to saying a daily prayer over nine days to a particular saint or higher spiritual entity. The first day usually begins on the Saint's Day, usually the day of their death. For me, this is May 22nd.

First Day

Saint Rita, I earnestly implore you to plead my cause before the throne of mercy.

You have been known as the "Saint of the Impossible." By your intercession, you have obtained from God many and great favors for those in urgent need of divine help.

I now ask you to obtain for me the gift of firm trust in the goodness of God; that I may always remember that God is a kind and generous

Father to me; that He always has a loving concern for my welfare.

Saint Rita, by your submission to God's will, obtain my request.

Say the: Our Father and Hail Mary.

Prayer

Oh God, who in Your infinite tenderness, have safeguarded the prayer of Your servant Rita, and grant to her supplication of that which is impossible to human foresight, skill and effort, in reward for her compassionate love and firm reliance on Your promises, have pity on our adversities and succor us in our calamities, that the unbeliever may know You are the recompense of the humble, the defense of the helpless, and the strength of those who trust in You, through Jesus Christ our Lord. Amen.

Second Day

Saint Rita, your life on Earth was one of many difficulties and severe temptations. It would have been an impossible life to live, but the Grace of God sustained you.

I now ask you to obtain for me the gift of always seeking the Grace of God; that I may be ever mindful of His promise to help me; that in temptation, my prayer may be: "Lord Save Me."

Say the: Our Father and Hail Mary

Third Day

Saint Rita, you were a model to your companions in your loyalty to obedience. You obeyed your parents, even at the cost of great personal sacrifice; you obeyed your husband, although he treated you poorly and abusively; as a nun you obeyed your Mother Superior in every detail of religious life.

I now ask you to obtain for me the spirit of obedience; that I may cheerfully obey any superiors I may have; and that I may always remember my Savior, Jesus Christ, and his spirit of obedience until death, for love of me.

Saint Rita, by your constant obedience, please hear my request.

Say the: Our Father and Hail Mary.

Fourth Day

Your parents were known as the "Peacemakers of God." Wherever there was discord, they entered that home and, by gentle words and prayers, established peace. You learned from them to treasure peace. Throughout your life, you imitated their example.

I now ask you to obtain for me the gift of peace – peace of a good conscience; peace of mind; peace in my home; peace at my work and with my companions. I ask my Savior to always grant me the peace He has guaranteed, particularly in distress and worry.

Saint Rita, by your love for peace, obtain my request.

Say the: Our Father and Hail Mary.

Fifth Day

Saint Rita, you gave to all an example of heroic virtue in your generous forgiving of those who injured you. When your husband was murdered, you openly proclaimed full forgiveness for the murderer and you constantly prayed for his conversion.

I now ask you to obtain for me the spirit of true forgiveness for those who injure me; that I may always remember the command of Our Lord: "Pray for your enemies, do good to them who hate you," that I may be ever mindful of His great promise: "Forgive, and you shall be forgiven."

Saint Rita, generous in forgiving, obtain my request.

Say the: Our Father and Hail Mary.

Sixth Day

Saint Rita, suffering and sorrow were your companions throughout life. Patiently and cheerfully you accepted every trial. You learned the secret of a happy life: to unite your sufferings to those of our Savior. The crucifix was ever before your eyes; from it you drew strength and consolation.

I now ask you to obtain for me the gift of patience in suffering; that I may ever remember that God permits only that amount of sorrow to enter my life which, with His Grace, I can bear; that in suffering, my prayer may always be: "Passion of Christ, strengthen me."

Saint Rita, by your compassion for the crucified Jesus, obtain my request.

Say the: Our Father and Hail Mary.

Seventh Day

Saint Rita, Jesus in the Blessed Sacrament was the mainstay of your life. You had learned from your mother to receive Him so reverently in Holy Communion. To our Lord in the Blessed Sacrament you united yourself, so that you showed in your life His promise: "He that eats My flesh abides in Me and I in him."

I now ask you to obtain for me a deep reverence for our Lord in the Blessed Sacrament; that I may worthily receive Him as often as possible; that I may frequently visit

114

Him in the Sacrament of His Love; that I may always treasure His Divine Presence.

Saint Rita, by your love for the Blessed Sacrament, obtain my request.

Say the: Our Father and Hail Mary.

Eighth Day

Saint Rita, from your own childhood you cultivated that spirit of prayer. You pondered on the meaning of the Our Father and Hail Mary; you filled your mind with the message of the gospels; you learned the secret of prayer – a humble conversation with God.

I now ask you to obtain for me the spirit of prayer; that I may always speak to God from my heart; that I

115

may ever remember that I live in the presence of God.

Saint Rita, by your spirit of prayer, obtain my request.

Say the: Our Father and Hail Mary.

Ninth Day

Saint Rita, throughout your life you were ever concerned with the practice of charity. You were meek and gentle; you were kind and compassionate; you did not spare yourself in bringing help to others.

I now ask you to obtain for me the spirit of charity; that I may always remember this is the greatest virtue; that I may ever strive to be kind in thought, word and deed; that I may, in all things, love others for the love of God.

Saint Rita, by your spirit of charity, obtain my request.

Say the: Our Father and Hail Mary.

Supplication to Saint Rita

Holy Patroness of those in need, Saint Rita, whose pleadings before our Divine Lord are favorably received; who has been called the advocate of the hopeless and impossible cases – be generous to your supplicants and show your power with God on their behalf. Be lavish in your favors now, as you have been in so many wonderful cases: for the greater glory of God, the spreading of your devotion, and the consolation of those who trust in you. Relying on your power of intercession before the Sacred Heart of Jesus, I ask of you:

_____.

Let Us Pray

O God, Who in Thy goodness, did bestow on Saint Rita abundant grace to love those who injured her; to have her heart ever devoted to Jesus Christ and her forehead sorely wounded from the thought of His intercession and merits, we also may forgive our enemies, and be so mindful of Jesus, sorrowful unto death, that we may obtain the reward promised to the meek of heart and to all who suffer patiently for His sake; Who livest and reignest forever and ever. Amen.

A Husband's Prayer

O, glorious Saint Rita, by the holiness of your life, you so influenced your husband that he conquered the harshness of his nature, and became a devoted husband and father. Pray that I may steadfastly follow the path of right reason and love. Never let me stray into the ways of selfishness and vice. Help me to always be an example of true spiritual life in word and deed. May I therefore become ever more worthy to reflect in my own family the example of Jesus Christ, of love, compassion, truth, support and eternal salvation. Amen.

A Wife's Prayer

O glorious Saint Rita, you fulfilled the duties of wedlock with loving fidelity through eighteen years of married life. Pray for me that I may bear never allow the evil one to turn my mind and heart to unholy designs. Help me to be faithful and devoted with sincere love and given to the care of my family in patience. Make me follow in your footsteps and exemplify love and peace. Amen.

For Patience and Sickness

O glorious Saint Rita, model of patience, I ask you by your love for your suffering Savior, which helped you to endure pain and sorrow patiently, to obtain for me the grace that I may accept my sickness willingly from the hands of God and be patient to the end. I desire, by practicing perfect patience, to be conformed to Christ in His suffering and that my suffering may become fruitful for eternal life. Amen.

Prayer for the Blessing of Children

O glorious Saint Rita, your coming into the world brought joy and happiness to the hearts of your parents, who had prayed for so long for a child. I pray now for the same favor. Obtain for me the joy of parenthood. I promise to accept the child as a sacred trust from the hands of God and to do everything to promote its eternal salvation. Amen.

Prayer for Spiritual Vocations

O glorious Saint Rita, you heard God's call for religious and spiritual life in your early youth and remained faithful to it through many years. Look down upon the many people whom God has marked for spiritual vocation. Help them to hear God's call and to remain faithful to His divine purpose. Let not worldly interests and pleasures obscure their minds and dull the tender feelings of their hearts, but keep awake in them the ideal of the Word of God. Amen.

Prayer of Bereavement

O glorious Saint Rita, you suffered the sorrows of bereavement at the death of your husband and children. Look upon me in my present sorrow at the loss of my loved one and obtain for me the grace of true Christian resignation and consolation. Amen.

Prayer for All Necessities

O glorious Saint Rita, who shared in the sorrowful passion of Our Lord Jesus Christ, obtain for me the grace to suffer with resignation the trials of this life and assist me in all necessities. Thank you for all your love and intercession. Amen.

Prayer for Students

O eternal and amazing God, Source of all creation and Source of all knowledge and wisdom, enlightenment and faith; design to infuse into my heart a spark of your own wisdom and knowledge; dissipate the darkness of my ignorance.

The inspired words You dictated speak of the eloquence You give to the tongues of children; please give me that power of speech, and put your words into my mouth. Grant me in learning a keen facility of retaining what I learn, and the talent of right interpretation.

123

O my Immaculate Mother, the Virgin and Mother Mary, seat of divine wisdom and love, and dear Saint Rita, Saint of the Impossible, give to us wisdom, love and the elimination of fear, so that I may obtain enlightenment and Christian perfection.

Through Christ our Lord. Amen.

The Driver's Prayer

Lord, grant me firm hands and vigilant eyes, so that my driving will not disturb the peace or bring suffering to others. I pray, Lord, also for those who are with me. Protect them from harm, from fire and accident.

Teach me to use my car for the welfare of others. Help me to understand that I must not sacrifice the beauty of creation—life itself—to the speed I desire. Teach me to travel with joy, making courtesy my companion along the road of life, mindful that life is your sacred gift. Saint Rita, please protect us. Amen.

Prayer for an Expectant Mother

Lord, God, Creator of all things, just and merciful, good and loving as no one else can be, you prepared the body and soul of the glorious Virgin Mary through the power of the Holy Spirit to be a worthy dwelling place for Thy Son, listen to the fervent prayer I make through the intercession of Saint Rita, our Saint of the Impossible, that the longing desire of my heart may be realized and no harm may befall the child in my womb. With Your compassionate hand, help me in my labor and may my baby see the light of day and grow to be a healthy child, born again to grace, and one day enjoy eternal life. I make this my prayer through Christ our Lord. Amen.

Prayer for Families

O God of mercy and peace, you gave to Saint Rita the grace to love even those who live by hatred and revenge. As you so graciously blessed her, I ask you to bless our family. Through the intercession of Saint Rita, model of patience and fortitude, bless and protect us from all selfish ways. Make us grow strong in the spirit of charity and forgiveness, and like your servant Saint Rita, may we be faithful peacemakers in our family, in our neighborhood, and in the world. Amen.

Hymn to Saint Rita

O glorious name, our own Saint Rita

O glorious name, sweet name of love.

Throughout the years, thy name forgotten

Thy children now thy grace implore

O glorious name, our own Saint Rita

O glorious name, sweet name of love.

What priceless gifts, what endless treasure

Now flowing from that boundless store

In all our joys, in all our sorrows

No prayers of ours shall thou ignore.

Bibliography

Butler, Alban. Lives of the Saints. TAN Books. 1995.

Cumming, Heather & Leffler, Karen. John of God: The Brazilian Healer Who's Touched the Lives of Millions. Atria Books. 2007.

Di Gregorio, Michael, OSA. The Precious Pearl: The Story of Saint Rita of Cascia. NY, New York: Alba House. 2002.

Hoever, Hugo. Lives of the Saints. Catholic Book Publishing Corp. 1988.

McAree, Francis, S.T.D. and Sheridan Patrick, D.D. Saint Rita, Saint of the Impossible. Canada: Catholic Book Publishing Corp. 1999.

Paoloni, Andrea. Saint Rita's Life and Prayers. Cascia: ST. RITA's Convent. 2000.

Paul, Tessa. The Illustrated World Encyclopedia of Saints. Lorenz Books. 2009.

Sicardo, Fr. Joseph, O.S.A., translated to English by Murphy, Fr. Dan J., St. Rita of Cascia, Saint of the Impossible. North Carolina: TAN Books. 1993.

Sanderson, Ruth. Saints, Lives and Illuminations. Eerdmans Books for Young Readers. 2010.